Summary

of

Sweet and Savory Fat Bombs
Martina Slajerova

Conversation Starters

By Paul Adams
Book Habits

Bonus Downloads
Get Free Books with __Any Purchase__ of Conversation Starters!

Every purchase comes with a FREE download!

Add spice to any conversation
Never run out of things to say
Spend time with those you love

Get it Now

or Click Here.

Scan Your Phone

Tips for Using Conversation Starters:

EVERY GOOD BOOK CONTAINS A WORLD FAR DEEPER THAN the surface of its pages. Questions herein are designed to bring us beneath the surface of the page and invite us into the world that lives on. These questions can be used to:

- Foster a deeper understanding of the book
- Promote an atmosphere of discussion for groups
- Assist in the study of the book, either individually or corporately
- Explore unseen realms of the book as never seen before

Table of Contents

Introducing *Sweet and Savory Fat Bombs*

*S*weet and Savory Fatbombs: 100 Delicious Treats for Fasts, Ketogenic, Paleo, and Low-Carb Diets* is a book written by keto and low-carb diet advocate Martina Slajerova.

The book features 100 snack recipes meant for people who follow paleo, keto, and low-carb diets. She features sweet treats that are low in carbs and savory snacks that do not cause your blood sugar to spike. She assures readers that there is a healthy way to enjoy ice cream, chocolate bars, and truffles without loading up on carbs. Slajerova had been following a low-carb diet for four years when she wrote the book. She says that her energy had never been better since she cut processed foods from her diet. She also feels that her new diet makes her feel like she is not dieting at all. She tells her readers that a low-carb diet will make one stop craving for sugary foods and enjoy whole foods instead. But she still enjoys sweets and snacks and this is the reason why she wrote this book. A sample of her fat bombs include Waldorf Salad fat bombs, Bacon and Guacamole fat bombs, and Almond and Cashew Butter fat bombs, Gingerbread Truffles, among many others.

In Chapter One, Slajerova defines what a keto diet is. It is a low-carbohydrate diet that's high in fat, moderate in protein, and low in carbs. She stresses the idea that our daily energy should be sourced from fats in order to bring about ketosis, a metabolic state which makes our bodies use fat as a source of energy instead of sugar. Our bodies will burn fat, not sugar. This causes our bodies to have fewer cravings and eat less. She says the quality of fats and proteins that one eats is important when doing the keto diet. Fat bombs are ideal snacks for keto diets because they are high in fats and low in protein and carbs. In Chapter Two, the author discusses the basics in creating fat bombs. She gives instructions on how to prepare nut and seed butter which are among her basic ingredients. Chapter Three features Sweet Fat Bombs. Chapter Four focuses on Frozen Fat Bombs, while Chapters Five and Six feature Liquid Fat Bombs, and Savory Fat bombs. A favorite chapter among readers is Chapter Three which shows recipes that prove "a sugar-free, keto-friendly diet is anything but boring!" The chapter includes Quick Orange Fat Bombs, Eggnog Truffles, Coconut candies, and Chocolate Avocado Truffles.

Beautiful photos of the recipes are included, with well-designed layouts. A list of the essential fat bomb ingredients is outlined in the first chapter, which includes activated nuts and seeds, coconut products, cacao and chocolate, dairy and dairy substitutes, sweeteners, raw eggs, among others.

The details of these products are explained to further identify their qualities and different kinds.

Instructions on how to activate nuts and seeds are included. Nutrition facts are included in the recipes. Critics cite the creative recipes in the last chapter which show how readers can make fat bombs out of sardines, salmon, bacon-eggs, and guacamole. Critics cite the square shape of the print book saying that it is awkward to hold and the print is hard to read. A reader says "using a lighter typeface for the actual recipe as opposed to the boldface used in the rest of the book also made it harder to read."

An Amazon review says the author's passion for creating recipes for a low-carb diet shows through her creations. Her recipes have helped the reviewer fulfill her cravings for sweets. The photographs were also lovingly done. A review done by mariammindbodyhealth.com says amazing recipes are combined with the fantastic layout and photos.

Another Amazon review cites the dairy-based recipes where substitutes are provided for the lactose-intolerant. The reviewer advises the lactose-intolerant readers to modify or leave out some ingredients. Another review repeats this concern, saying that more dairy-free options could have been added to the book. A Goodreads review says the book offers good recipes for parties. The reviewer does not use artificial sweeteners, however, and says many of the recipes include such sweeteners. Another Goodreads review echoes this artificial sweetener concern and says using them "contradicts what the high-fat low carb diet is all about." A reader says that many people fail at dieting because these diets are restrictive. Slajerova's book, however, provides her "the pleasure and joy of eating what feels forbidden, with all the benefits that add to a successful keto diet! " She also thinks the recipes are written clearly and are easy to follow. Another reader cites the "interesting, delicious, and uncomplicated recipes." She likes the idea that these are not only used for fat bombs but can be used in smoothies, appetizers, butter, among others. She will recommend the book to her keto dieting friends.

Sweet and Savory Fatbombs is written by Martina Slajerova, the bestselling author of *The Keto Diet Cookbook* and *Quick Keto Meals in 30 Minutes or Less*.

Discussion Questions

"Get Ready to Enter a New World"

Tip: Begin with questions dealing with broader issues to ensure ample time for quality discussions. Read through all discussion questions before engaging.

question 1

In Chapter One, Slajerova defines what a keto diet is. It is a low-carbohydrate diet that's high in fat, moderate in protein, and low in carbs. She stresses the idea that our daily energy should be sourced from fats in order to bring about ketosis, a metabolic state which makes our bodies use fat as a source of energy instead of sugar. Fat bombs are ideal snacks for keto diets. How are fat bombs ideal for a low-carb, keto diet?

~~~

question 2

In Chapter Two, the author discusses the basics in creating fat bombs. She gives instructions on how to prepare nut and seed butter which are among her basic ingredients. Why do we need to know how to prepare nut and seed butter? How are seeds and nuts related to fat bombs?

~~~

question 3

Chapter Three features Sweet Fat Bombs. Chapter Four focuses on Frozen Fat Bombs, while Chapters Five and Six feature Liquid Fat Bombs, and Savory Fat bombs. Which chapter is your favorite? Why?

~~~

question 4

A favorite chapter among readers is Chapter Three which shows recipes that prove "a sugar-free, keto-friendly diet is anything but boring!" The chapter includes Quick Orange Fat Bombs, Eggnog Truffles, Coconut candies, and Chocolate Avocado Truffles. Which is your favorite recipe in chapter three? Why?

~~~

question 5

Beautiful photos of the recipes are included, with well-designed layouts. How would you describe the photos? How does the layout complement the photos?

~~~

question 6

The book features 100 snack recipes meant for people who follow paleo, keto, and low-carb diets. She features sweet treats that are low in carbs and savory snacks that do not cause your blood sugar to spike. How are the 100 recipes distributed among the chapters? Is there an even distribution? Do some chapters have more or fewer recipes? Why do you think the number of recipes is distributed this way?

~~~

question 7

She assures readers that there is a healthy way to enjoy ice cream, chocolate bars, and truffles without loading up on carbs. Slajerova had been following a low-carb diet for four years when she wrote the book. She says that her energy had never been better since she cut processed foods from her diet. Do you feel assured that eating her fat bombs can make you healthier? Why? Why not?

~~~

question 8

She tells her readers that a low-carb diet will make one stop craving for sugary foods and enjoy whole foods instead. But she still enjoys sweets and snacks and this is the reason why she wrote this book. Do you crave sugar? Do you think her recipes will help solve your cravings? Why? Why not?

~~~

question 9

A list of the essential fat bomb ingredients is outlined in the first chapter, which includes activated nuts and seeds, coconut products, cacao and chocolate, dairy and dairy substitutes, sweeteners, raw eggs, among others. The details of these products are explained to further identify their qualities and different kinds. Do you find this part helpful? In what way?

~~~

question 10

A large number of her recipes include nuts and seeds. Instruction on how to activate nuts and seeds is included. Why do we need to activate nuts and seeds? What happens if we don't?

~~~

question 11

Nutrition facts are included in the recipes. Do you think citing nutrition facts is important? Why? Will there be readers who are not particularly interested in the nutrition aspect?

~~~

question 12

Critics cite the creative recipes in the last chapter which show how readers can make fat bombs out of sardines, salmon, bacon-eggs, and guacamole. Why do they find this part creative and unique? Do you find the recipes interesting as well? Why? Why not?

~~~

question 13

The print copy of the book is square shaped. Some readers do not think its is a good form for the book. It is accordingly hard to handle. Do you think this is a good idea? Why? Why not?

~~~

question 14

According to a reader, the book "uses a lighter typeface for the actual recipe as opposed to the boldface used in the rest of the book..." What is the effect of this kind of design? Do you like it? Why? Why not?

~~~

question 15

The photographs were lovingly done. A review done by mariammindbodyhealth.com says amazing recipes are combined with the fantastic layout and photos. Why do recipe books normally feature great photography? What about recipe books that make them ideal for photographs?

question 16

An Amazon review says the author's passion for creating recipes for a low-carb diet shows through her creations. Her recipes have helped the reviewer fulfill her cravings for sweets. Can you cite a particular part in the book where the author's passion shows through? How does your example show her passion?

~~~

question 17

A review done by mariammindbodyhealth.com along with other readers' reviews say amazing recipes are combined with the fantastic layout and photos. Do you agree? Do you think people will buy the book just for the photos and beautiful design? Why? Why not?

~~~

~~~

question 18

An Amazon review cites the dairy-based recipes where substitutes are provided for the lactose-intolerant. The reviewer advises the lactose-intolerant readers to modify or leave out some ingredients. Another review repeats this concern, saying that more dairy-free options could have been added to the book. Why are readers concerned about dairy? Is dairy part of your diet? Why? Why not?

~~~

question 19

A Goodreads review says the book offers good recipes for parties. The reviewer does not use artificial sweeteners, however, and says many of the recipes include such sweeteners. Another Goodreads review echoes this artificial sweetener concern and says using them "contradicts what the high-fat low carb diet is all about." Do you think artificial sweeteners should not have been included? Why? Why not?

~~~

question 20

A reader says that many people fail at dieting because these diets are restrictive. Slajerova's book, however, provides her "the pleasure and joy of eating what feels forbidden, with all the benefits that add to a successful keto diet! " How do you feel about eating the forbidden? Does the book help you deal with forbidden food?

~~~

Introducing the Author

Martina Slajerova was diagnosed with Hashimoto's disease in 2011. The disease attacked her immune system and made her constantly tired. Despite following a healthy lifestyle, eating a balanced diet that was low in to prevent clogging her arteries, and eating fruits, vegetables, whole grains, with a minimal intake of meat and dairy, she still found herself low in energy. She decided to do her own research, stop dieting, and find another way to get well. She stopped taking sugar, processed foods, and grains. She also started her ketogenic lifestyle. Her health started to improve. Convinced of the healing power of the keto diet, she and her partner created an application that tracks and plans low carb recipes, called KetoDiet. In 2012, she launched the KetoDiet blog which features whole foods-based, ketogenic, low-carb recipes and lifestyle. The app has since become one of the most popular apps and the blog has reached over two million monthly guests. Slajerova started writing books about the keto and low-carb diet " to help people follow a healthy diet and to show them that this way of eating doesn't have to be complicated or boring," she writes in her blog. Her published books are The KetoDiet Cookbook, Sweet & Savory Fat Bombs, Quick Keto Meals in 30 Minutes or Less, and Keto Slow Cooker & One-Pot Meals.

Slajerova stresses that her keto lifestyle is not limited to losing weight. It is, more importantly, having a healthy lifestyle. "My mission is to help you reach your goals, whether it's your dream weight or simply eating healthy food," she says in her blog. When she first started shifting to a low-carb diet, she found it hard to quit sugar and grains. The first three to four weeks were hardest, she says, but once she got over this period, she found it easier to adjust to a low-carb diet. She calls herself a science geek who uses her research and experience to provide advice to people who want to know more about the keto diet. Her recipes are not just focused on the number of calories but on the delicious and healthy ingredients that comprise the recipes.

"Once you make the decision to go low-carb—and commit to it—you'll soon stop missing sugar and grains, and you'll enjoy eating whole foods without being plagued by cravings," she says in the introduction to her book *Sweet and Savory Fat Bombs.*

Slajerova lives in the United Kingdom. She has an Economics degree and used to work in auditing. Aside from her passion for healthy food, nutrition, regular exercise, and low-carb diet, she is also a photography enthusiast. This is reflected in her cookbooks which feature photos that have earned raves from readers. Her blog posts and her recipes have been featured in *Glamour, BuzzFeed, HuffPost*

Healthy Living, and *Cosmopolitan*, and in many other sites that feature low-carb diets.

Slajerova's work is highly regarded by medical doctors and scientists. Alex Pearlman, a cancer biologist who does research on ketogenic diet and cancer at the Albert Einstein College of Medicine says she has made "valuable contributions to the low-carb community." Additionally, "her involvement in the cancer research project run by our team extend beyond simply helping people follow a healthy low-carb diet." He recommends her cookbooks to all those who are interested in healthy living. Professor of radiology Eugene J. Fine at the Albert Einstein College of Medicine says "Martina's work, including her blog, book, and apps, have been real gems for the low-carb community." He adds that her "real-food approach and attention to detail sets her work apart from many others." Franziska Spritzler, RD, CDE who wrote *The Low Carb Dietitian's Guide to Health and Beauty* appreciates Slajerova's talent and innovation in creating her blog, app, and books. She cites Slajerova's "accurate, reliable information" and recommends her work "to people interested in following a healthy, carbohydrate-restricted lifestyle."

Bonus Downloads

*Get Free Books with **<u>Any Purchase</u>** of* Conversation Starters!

Every purchase comes with a FREE download!

Add spice to any conversation
Never run out of things to say
Spend time with those you love

Get it Now

<u>or Click Here.</u>

Scan Your Phone

Fireside Questions

"What would you do?"

Tip: These questions can be a fun exercise as it spurs creativity among the readers by allowing alternate scene endings and "if this was you" questions.

question 21

When she got sick, she decided to do her own research, stop dieting, and find a way to get well. She stopped taking sugar, processed foods, and grains. She also started her ketogenic lifestyle. Her health started to improve. Slajerova stresses that her keto lifestyle is not limited to losing weight. It is, more importantly, having a healthy lifestyle. Why is the keto lifestyle primarily a healthy practice? Of the people you know who are doing the keto diet, what is their main motivation?

~~~

question 22

Convinced of the healing power of the keto diet, she and her partner created an application that tracks and plans low carb recipes, called KetoDiet. In 2012, she launched the KetoDiet blog which features whole foods-based, ketogenic, low-carb recipes and lifestyle. How successful are her keto-related endeavors? Why do you think these are successful?

~~~

question 23

When she first started shifting to a low-carb diet, she found it hard to quit sugar and grains. The first three to four weeks were hardest, she says, but once she got over this period, she found it easier to adjust to a low-carb diet. Why was it hard for her to quit sugar and grains? How does the body normally react to quitting sugar and grains?

~~~

question 24

Slajerova's work is highly regarded by medical doctors and scientists. Alex Pearlman, a cancer biologist who does research on ketogenic diet and cancer at the Albert Einstein College of Medicine is one of them. What do the doctors and scientists say about her work?

question 25

"Once you make the decision to go low-carb—and commit to it—you'll soon stop missing sugar and grains, and you'll enjoy eating whole foods without being plagued by cravings," she says in the introduction to her book Sweet and Savory Fat Bombs. Do you find this true to your experience? How would you describe your shift to keto diet?

~~~

question 26

Slajerova started writing books about the keto and low-carb diet " to help people follow a healthy diet and to show them that this way of eating doesn't have to be complicated or boring," she writes in her blog. Her published books are The KetoDiet Cookbook, Sweet & Savory Fat Bombs, Quick Keto Meals in 30 Minutes or Less, and Keto Slow Cooker & One-Pot Meals. If you are her, what other keto diet book would you be writing soon? Why?

~~~

question 27

She calls herself a science geek who uses her research and experience to provide advice to people who want to know more about the keto diet. Her recipes are not just focused on the number of calories but on the delicious and healthy ingredients that comprise the recipes. Slajerova stresses that her keto lifestyle is not limited to losing weight. It is, more importantly, having a healthy lifestyle. If she did keto not because she was sick but because she wanted to lose weight, how different would her blogs and books be?

~~~

question 28

Martina Slajerova was diagnosed with Hashimoto's disease in 2011. The disease has attacked her immune system and made her constantly tired. Despite following a healthy lifestyle, eating a balanced diet that was low in to prevent clogging her arteries, and eating fruits, vegetables, whole grains, with a minimal intake of meat and dairy, she still found herself low in energy. If you are her, how would you deal with the disease if the keto diet has not yet been discovered?

~~~

question 29

A Goodreads review says the book offers good recipes for parties. The reviewer does not use artificial sweeteners, however, and says many of the recipes include such sweeteners. Another Goodreads review echoes this artificial sweetener concern and says using them "contradicts what the high-fat low carb diet is all about." If you are the author, how would you change your recipes to accommodate this concern?

~~~

question 30

Critics cite the square shape of the print book saying that it is awkward to hold and the print is hard to read. A reader says "using a lighter typeface for the actual recipe as opposed to the boldface used in the rest of the book also made it harder to read." If you will direct the design for the book, how would you do it?

~~~

Quiz Questions

"Ready to Announce the Winners?"

Tip: Create a leaderboard and track scores to see who gets the most correct answers. Winners required. Prizes optional.

quiz question 1

In Chapter _____, Slajerova defines what a keto diet is. It is a low-carbohydrate diet that's high in fat, moderate in protein, and low in carbs. She stresses the idea that our daily energy should be sourced from fats in order to bring about ketosis. 2. Fat bombs are ideal snacks for keto diets because they are high in fats and low in _____ and carbs.

~~~

~~~

quiz question 2

Fat bombs are ideal snacks for keto diets because they are high in fats and low in _____ and carbs.

~~~

quiz question 3

A favorite chapter among readers is Chapter Three which shows recipes that prove "a _____-free, keto-friendly diet is anything but boring!" The chapter includes Quick Orange Fat Bombs, Eggnog Truffles, Coconut candies, and Chocolate Avocado Truffles.

~~~

quiz question 4

True or False: A list of the essential fat bomb ingredients are outlined in the first chapter, which includes activated nuts and seeds, coconut products, cacao and chocolate, dairy and dairy substitutes, sweeteners, raw eggs, among others.

~~~

~~~

quiz question 5

True or False: Nutrition facts are included in the recipes.

~~~

quiz question 6

True or False: She stresses the idea that our daily energy should be sourced from protein in order to bring about ketosis, a metabolic state which makes our bodies use fat as a source of energy instead of sugar.

quiz question 7

True or False: She says the quality of fats and proteins that one eats is important when doing the keto diet.

~~~

~~~

quiz question 8

Martina Slajerova was diagnosed with _____ disease in 2011. The disease attacked her immune system and made her constantly tired.

~~~

quiz question 9

Convinced of the healing power of the keto diet, she and her partner created an application that tracks and plans low carb recipes, called _____.

~~~

quiz question 10

Slajerova's work is highly regarded by medical doctors and scientists. Alex Pearlman, a cancer biologist who does research on ketogenic diet and cancer at the _____says she has made "valuable contributions to the low-carb community."

~~~

quiz question 11

True or False: In 2012, she launched the KetoDiet blog which features whole foods-based, ketogenic, low-carb recipes and lifestyle.

~~~

~~~

quiz question 12

True or False: Slajerova stresses that her keto lifestyle is not limited to losing weight. It is, more importantly, having a healthy lifestyle. "My mission is to help you reach your goals, whether it's your dream weight or simply eating healthy food," she says in her blog.

~~~

Quiz Answers

1. One
2. protein
3. sugar
4. True
5. True
6. False
7. True
8. Hashimoto's
9. KetoDiet
10. Albert Einstein College of Medicine
11. True
12. True

Ways to Continue Your Reading

EVERY month, our team runs through a wide selection of books to pick the best titles for readers and reading groups, and promotes these titles to our thousands of readers – sometimes with free downloads, sale dates, and additional brochures.

Click here to sign up for these benefits.

If you have not yet read the original work or would like to read it again, you can purchase the original book here.

Bonus Downloads
*Get Free Books with **<u>Any Purchase</u>** of* Conversation Starters!

Every purchase comes with a FREE download!

Add spice to any conversation
Never run out of things to say
Spend time with those you love

Get it Now

<u>or Click Here.</u>

Scan Your Phone

On the Next Page...

If you found this book helpful to your discussions and rate it a 4 or 5, please write us a review on the next page.

Any length would be fine but we'd appreciate hearing you more! We'd be very encouraged.

Till next time,

BookHabits

"Loving Books is Actually a Habit"

Lightning Source UK Ltd.
Milton Keynes UK
UKHW040616071019
351149UK00001B/166/P